# UNSOLVED MYSTERIES

Reading and discussion for intermediate-level students

GEORGE P McCALLUM

Nelson

**Thomas Nelson and Sons Ltd**
Nelson House   Mayfield Road
Walton-on-Thames   Surrey
KT12 5PL   UK

51 York Place
Edinburgh
EH1 3JD   UK

**Thomas Nelson (Hong Kong) Ltd**
Toppan Building 10/F
22A Westlands Road
Quarry Bay   Hong Kong


© George P McCallum 1990

First published by Thomas Nelson and Sons Ltd 1990

ISBN 0-17-555897-3

NPN 9 8 7 6 5 4 3 2 1

Printed in Hong Kong

**Acknowledgements**
Photographs
The publisher would like to thank the following for kind permission to reproduce copyright photographs:
Ronald Grant, *page 10*; the Mansell Collection, *page 15*; Tony Stone Associates, *page 20*; Columbia Pictures, *page 46*.

Illustrations
Gabrielle Morton, *cover*; David Sawyers, *pages 5*, *25*, *30*, *35*, Ian Foulis and Associates, page 41.

# Contents

# Introduction

Most people like a mystery and like playing detective; the challenge of solving a crime or other problem is always fun. *Unsolved Mysteries* is a book designed for intermediate-level students of English that gives you such an opportunity. It contains some real-life mysteries, situations for which no solutions have ever been found (although many people have tried). Now you have your chance!

Apart from providing you with an enjoyable challenge, this book offers practice in the four skills of English: reading, writing, listening and speaking, with emphasis on reading and speaking.

*Unsolved Mysteries* is divided into ten lessons, each with the following format:
— The mystery
— A comprehension check on the reading in the form of true/false statements, multiple-choice questions and open-ended sentences.
— Language practice. This consists of a vocabulary and phrasal verb exercise which provides contextualisation and practice of some of the words and phrasal verbs in the reading, and a grammar point used in the reading, with a brief explanation of that point as well as an exercise based on it.
— Discussion. This is a discussion of the mystery, with an opportunity to solve it.
— Writing. This final section of the lesson allows you to express your own thoughts about the mystery. You may be asked to write a letter about it or to be a reporter writing an article for your newspaper, and so on.

As part of the language practice has to do with phrasal verbs it might be a good idea to refresh your memory as to what a phrasal verb is and how it is used: actually a phrasal verb is a 'miniature idiom' of two, sometimes three, words: a verb plus one or more prepositions. Like idioms, the words in a phrasal verb mean something quite different when taken together than they do individually. The words *look up*, when taken individually, simply mean *raise your eyes upwards.* As a phrasal verb, however, these two words mean something quite different: *find information in a reference book* or *visit unexpectedly.* There is often very little relationship between the meaning of the individual words and their combination in a phrasal verb.

Finally, a word about the mysteries themselves. The readings here are brief and give only the information necessary for the class to have an interesting discussion. If you would like to know more about any of them, lots of books and articles have been published on all the subjects included here. There are also hundreds of other unsolved mysteries that you might want to read about, too and try to solve!

# 1. THE LOCH NESS MONSTER :
## real or imaginary

Have you heard of the Loch Ness Monster?
If so, what have you heard?
Do you think this creature really exists
in Scotland's largest lake?

# The mystery

One afternoon in April 1933, as John Mackay and his wife drove along the newly-constructed road at the edge of Loch Ness, Mrs Mackay, looking across the waters of Scotland's biggest lake, suddenly cried out, 'John! What's that?'

'Where?'

'Out there!' She pointed to the centre of the lake. Its usually quiet surface was strangely disturbed and covered with foam. Her husband stopped the car. Suddenly a huge creature appeared. The Mackays stared as it moved about in the water, going under, then popping up again. Finally, after a few minutes, it disappeared under the water and the lake became calm once more.

That was the first appearance in modern times of the Loch Ness Monster, the name which was given to it by a newspaper reporter. Later, this timid, harmless creature became affectionately known as Nessie.

Since the Mackays' experience with the mysterious animal in 1933, more than 3,000 other people claim that they have seen Nessie. Some of them believe that the lake is inhabited by ten, twenty or more of these creatures. The interesting thing is that a similar description of Nessie is given by almost everyone:

Length    — about fifty feet
Body    — thirty feet long, twelve feet around the middle
Head    — very small, compared with the body
Neck    — from four to seven feet long
Skin    — grey
Flippers    — two small ones at the front, two large ones at the back
Tail    — short and flat

Although the Mackays are the first people in modern times to see the Monster, about 1400 years ago St Columba, the man who brought Christianity to Scotland, was supposed to have seen a 'water monster' in Loch Ness. Little or no reference was made to it during the next 500 years, although in the nineteenth century an occasional mention was made in books and newspapers.

Why is it that since 1933 many people claim to have seen Nessie but, as far as is known, very few before then? One explanation is that shortly before that day in 1933 when the Mackays saw the Monster, a new road was constructed beside Loch Ness. In order to build the road the engineers blasted tons of rock into the lake. This evidently destroyed the animals' underwater home and forced them to swim about the lake in search of a new place to live. They rose to the surface with greater frequency after that.

If we assume that a 'monster' really exists in Loch Ness, what is it and how did it get there?

We are told by experts that Nessie may be a descendant of the plesiosaurs, creatures that lived over seven million years ago. Geologists say that Loch Ness was once a part of the sea; then, during the Ice Age, it was closed off by glaciers and a lake was formed. Therefore, it is possible that the original monster family was caught in the new lake, unable to leave. Somehow the monsters survived and, to this day, their descendants continue to inhabit Loch Ness.

## C ▷ What do scientists think about the Loch Ness Monster?

Just as there are people who believe in the Loch Ness Monster there are non-believers, too. Many of these are prominent scientists who demand further evidence. In spite of many eye-witness stories and remarkable photographs, scientists simply laugh off the idea that an unknown animal exists in Loch Ness. Here are some of their reasons:

— What people see on the surface of the lake are floating logs.
— Mass hallucination – the power of suggestion – has influenced people who say they have seen Nessie.
— The Monster is fiction, nothing more than propaganda put out by the Scottish Tourist Board.
— What people see are large otters.
— The claims are false ones, made by people who want to see their names in the newspapers.
— The pictures are photographs which have been cleverly touched up.

Here are some of the counter-arguments made by the pro-Nessie people:

— Logs could not move in the water the way the Monster does.
— The Scottish Tourist Board has never exploited Nessie in any way.
— Even a large otter could not disturb the surface of the water as Nessie does.
— Many highly-respected individuals have accepted the existence of an unknown creature in the lake; some even admit they have seen Nessie.
— Not everyone who claims to have seen the Monster is interested in publicity for himself/herself.

The search for Nessie goes on. Perhaps one day there will be sufficient proof that a monster does – or does not – exist in Loch Ness. Until now, however, that is not the case.

## Comprehension check

Look back at the reading and find information to complete these sentences.

1 Scotland's largest inland body of water is _____ .
2 In this century the Loch Ness Monster was first seen in _____ .
3 The Monster is affectionately called _____ .
4 Since 1933 the number of people who claim they have seen the Monster is about _____ .
5 St Columba was famous for _____ .
6 A plesiosaur is _____ .
7 According to geologists, Loch Ness was formed by _____ .
8 Scientists say that pictures taken of the Monster are _____ .
9 Pro-monster people say the logs in the lake _____ .
10 Supposedly some people make false statements about seeing the Monster because _____ .

# Language practice

## 1 Vocabulary

Here is some vocabulary from the text. You can deduce the meanings of these words from their context in the reading. In the left-hand column are the words from the reading; on the right are their definitions. Match the words with the definitions. The first one has been done for you.

| | | | | |
|---|---|---|---|---|
| 1 | foam (*l. 6*) **k** | a | say that something is true |
| 2 | huge (*l. 7*) | b | used explosives to break up rock |
| 3 | stared (*l. 7*) | c | person who sees something happen |
| 4 | claim (*l. 14*) | d | parts of a tree (cut into pieces by people) |
| 5 | flippers (*l. 22*) | e | many people seeing something which is not there |
| 6 | blasted (*l. 32*) | | |
| 7 | glacier (*l. 40*) | f | looked long and hard at something |
| 8 | eye-witness (*l. 46*) | g | extremely large |
| 9 | logs (*l. 49*) | h | limbs (like arms and legs) used by sea animals for swimming |
| 10 | mass hallucination (*l. 50*) | i | mass of ice moving down a mountain |
| 11 | otters (*l. 54*) | j | fur-covered water animals |
| | | k | white mass of bubbles on top of water |

## 2 Phrasal verbs

These phrasal verbs also come from the text. Match them with their definitions.

| | | | | |
|---|---|---|---|---|
| 1 | pop up (*l. 8*) | a | dismiss something as a joke |
| 2 | laugh off (*l. 47*) | b | produce |
| 3 | put out (*l. 52*) | c | continue |
| 4 | touch up (*l. 57*) | d | appear suddenly |
| 5 | go on (*l. 66*) | e | change appearance of something (a picture) |

## 3 Grammar: the passive

Look at this example:
Active: *The Mackays saw the monster.*
Passive: *The monster was seen by the Mackays.*

It is often possible to put a verb phrase in either the active or passive voice, according to the focus of the sentence.
In the active voice the subject performs the action.
In the passive voice the subject receives the action.
In the passive the verb *to be* is used with a past participle: *is said*, *were written*, *will be offered*.

### Exercise

Find ten uses of the passive voice in the reading and change them to the active voice, for example:
*A similar description of Nessie is given by almost everyone.*
*Almost everyone gives a similar description of Nessie.*

## Discussion

Your teacher will give you instructions on how to do this part of the lesson.

## Writing

What do *you* think? Is there a strange creature in Loch Ness? Write a paragraph of about 40 to 60 words giving your personal opinion.

# 2. ATLANTIS :

## is it only a legend ?

What do you know about Atlantis?
Dictionaries describe it as a legendary island
located in the Atlantic Ocean west of Gibraltar.
One day there was a terrible explosion
and it disappeared into the sea.
Was Atlantis a legendary island
or was it real?

METROSCOPE AND METROCOLOR

METRO-GOLDWYN-MAYER presents IN METROSCOPE AND METROCOLOR A GEORGE PAL PRODUCTION
ATLANTIS THE LOST CONTINENT Ⓐ starring ANTHONY HALL · JOYCE TAYLOR · JOHN DALL
Screenplay by DANIEL MAINWARING    Based on a play by SIR GERALD HARGREAVES    Produced and Directed by GEORGE PAL

# The mystery

## Where did Plato
## get his information about Atlantis?

It all started with the Greek philosopher, Plato. About 347 BC in two of his famous dialogues, Plato described a prosperous continent inhabited by people of great learning and culture. This continent, or island, was located beyond the 'Pillars of Hercules', which today we know as the Straits of Gibraltar. One day in 9600 BC, according to Plato, the island was destroyed by a volcanic explosion and a huge tidal wave. Overnight it sank to the bottom of the ocean. Only a few people escaped. The name Plato used in his dialogues for this island was Atlantis.

The story of the lost continent, as it is often called, was one told originally by a Greek statesman named Solon. He had heard of the island during a trip to Egypt in the sixth century BC and he found out all he could about it. What Plato wrote two centuries later was based on Solon's findings.

For thousands of years Plato's story of Atlantis was the only one; no one else wrote about it. The two dialogues were full of descriptive detail about the island and many of Plato's fellow Greeks were convinced the story was true. Others, however, including Plato's famous pupil, Aristotle, were not convinced. They did not go along with Plato but said it was an invention he used to illustrate his philosophy. Plato insisted that his account of Atlantis was completely authentic.

B

## Why are the
## Mayan and Incan civilizations mentioned here?

Since Plato's time millions of words have been written about Atlantis. There is a wide variety of opinion, however, about the location of the island and the exact date that it blew up and sank into the sea. Some authorities on the subject claim that it was located beneath the Azores and that these Portuguese islands in the Atlantic are the tops of mountains on Atlantis. This coincides with what Plato believed. Others feel it is farther south, under the Canary Islands.

Certain French archaeologists have announced that the Sahara Desert in North Africa was once covered by an inland sea and that by digging in the sand of the desert we will find Atlantis.

Spanish authorities on Atlantis insist that it is somewhere off the coast of Spain. Russian scientists tell us that the lost continent is in the Caspian Sea. There are many other fascinating theories, too. They differ in many ways but all agree on one basic point: long ago there existed a continent that blew up one day and disappeared beneath the waves of the ocean.

In 1882 an American named Ignatius T Donnelly gathered together all the information he could find about the mysterious island and published it in *Atlantis: The Antediluvian World*. Today Donnelly's book is still considered the 'bible' of Atlantis. The lost island, he reported, was where all the civilisations of the world, from Egyptian to Incan, originated. Survivors of the catastrophe in 9600 BC fled to the lands east and west. Some of them reached what is now America. There exists the belief among some people that Indians living in the Americas are descendants of these survivors. The Mayan and Incan cultures, according to this belief,

40 developed from the original civilisation of Atlantis. Incan and Mayan folktales relate the story of a people who escaped to America from a terrible disaster in a distant land.

## C  What caused the Minoan Empire to lose its power?

45 Early in the twentieth century attention turned to yet another explanation of Atlantis: Santorini, an island in the Aegean Sea. In ancient times this was called Thera and was part of the Minoan Empire. Scholars note similarities between Atlantis and the Minoan civilisation, which was centred at Knossos on the island of Crete. This was a powerful empire until about 1400 BC when a disastrous explosion caused much of Santorini to disappear into the sea. The tidal wave that followed reached Crete, destroying much of its coastline. This weakened the
50 Minoan Empire, which depended on sea trade. It never got back its former strength as a Mediterranean power.

A great difference in time can be seen here. According to Solon's account Atlantis disappeared in 9600 BC, but Santorini was destroyed in 1400 BC. There is a simple explanation for this great difference: Solon read the numerical symbols in the Egyptian records incorrectly. He read 100 as 1000. If we remove one zero we
55 can then read every number in Solon's story of Atlantis quite differently; the destruction of Atlantis thus took place about 900 years before Solon's time, not 9000 years; this places the tragic event in the fifteenth century BC, which is when Santorini was destroyed.

## D  What is David Zink's theory?

60 More recently an American visionary, Edgar Cayce, looked into the past and said he saw Atlantis. Although he had never read Plato's dialogues his description of the lost continent was similar to the one written 2300 years before in Athens. Cayce said that in his vision he saw Atlantis located near North Bimini, an island in the Bahamas. He predicted that in 1968 or 1969 some temples of the ancient
65 kingdom would be found there.

In 1968 a deep-sea diver, J Manson Valentine, came upon the ruins of some ancient buildings while swimming underwater off the coast of North Bimini. Since then other divers have explored the area. They declare that the 'buildings' Valentine saw were not made by man but were formed by nature.
70 In 1975 and again in 1977 expeditions conducted by David Zink in the same area brought blocks of stone to the surface. Zink insisted that because of the way these blocks had been formed and placed one on the top of the other, they could only be man-made. Until now no one has been able to dispute this theory.

Where Atlantis was located has been the subject of many arguments, but, for
75 the moment all that has been claimed, either for or against the existence of Atlantis, from Plato's day to the present, has been speculation. The mystery of the lost continent remains unsolved.

# Comprehension check

Look back at the reading and find information to fill the gaps in these sentences.

1 A Greek named _____ first brought the story of Atlantis from Egypt.
2 Plato's pupil, _____ , did not believe that Atlantis existed.
3 Some authorities believe that the _____ are the tops of mountains on Atlantis.
4 French archaeologists think that Atlantis lies beneath the _____ .
5 _____ say it is in the Caspian Sea.
6 A book by Ignatius T Donnelly is considered the _____ of Atlantis.
7 Santorini is an island in the Aegean Sea that was formerly named _____ .
8 The Minoan civilisation was centred at Knossos, on the island of _____ .
9 Edgar Cayce believed Atlantis was located near _____ , in the Bahama Islands.
10 David Zink brought _____ of stone to the surface of the water which, he said, were man made.

# Language practice

## 1 Vocabulary

Here is some vocabulary from the text. You can deduce the meanings of these words from their context in the reading. In the left-hand column are the words from the reading; on the right are their definitions. Match the words with the definitions. The first one has been done for you.

| | | | |
|---|---|---|---|
| 1 | straits (*l. 4*) **c** | a | ran away |
| 2 | tidal wave (*l. 6*) | b | under |
| 3 | sank (*l. 6*) | c | narrow water passage connecting two seas |
| 4 | authentic (*l. 17*) | | |
| 5 | beneath (*l. 21*) | d | disappear under the surface of the water |
| 6 | fled (*l. 36*) | | |
| 7 | visionary (*l. 60*) | e | argue about |
| 8 | diver (*l. 66*) | f | true/real |
| 9 | dispute (*l. 73*) | g | big, destructive movement of water in the ocean |
| 10 | speculation (*l. 76*) | | |
| | | h | opinion based on guessing |
| | | i | someone who can see into the future |
| | | j | person who swims underwater |

## 2 Phrasal verbs

These phrasal verbs also come from the text. Match them with their definitions.

| | | | |
|---|---|---|---|
| 1 | find out (*l. 10*) | a | find by accident |
| 2 | go along with (*l. 16*) | b | take possession again |
| 3 | blow up (*l. 20*) | c | agree with |
| 4 | get back (*l. 50*) | d | discover |
| 5 | come upon (*l. 66*) | e | explode |

## 3 Grammar: noun clauses

*What Plato wrote two centuries later was based on Solon's findings.*
*Where Atlantis was located has been the subject of many arguments.*

A noun clause is a dependent clause that is used as a noun (subject or object of the verb). It is usually found at the beginning or end of the sentence but can also be elsewhere in the sentence. It is often introduced by one of the following pronouns: *who, what, which, whom, whose, whoever, whichever, whatever, where, when, how, why, that.*

### Exercise

Use the appropriate pronoun (*what, that, who*, etc.) to fill the gaps in these sentences, for example:
*Most of the Greeks believed <u>what</u> Plato wrote about Atlantis.*

1 Plato insisted _____ the story of Atlantis was true.
2 Aristotle was one of the Greeks _____ did not believe Plato's story.
3 Authorities argue about _____ Atlantis is located.
4 _____ Aristotle did not believe the story of Atlantis is not clear.
5 No one really knows _____ Atlantis sank into the sea; some people say it was 9600 BC.
6 But _____ Atlantis was destroyed is not a mystery: it disappeared in a terrible explosion.
7 David Zink discovered blocks of stone in the sea _____ , he believes, are man made.
8 _____ has been said about Atlantis up till now is only speculation.

# Discussion

Your teacher will give you instructions on how do this part of the lesson.

# Writing

You are a newspaper reporter. The town where you live is on a sea coast. A deep-sea diver has discovered the ruins of an ancient city near the coast. Archaeologists believe it could be Atlantis. Write a short article about the discovery, beginning 'Ruins of an ancient city were discovered yesterday near the coast of . . .'

# 3. THE *MARY CELESTE* :
## why did the people on board disappear

Does the name *Mary Celeste* mean anything to you?
One of the most unusual mysteries of the sea
is about this nineteenth-century sailing ship
that one day left New York for Genoa, Italy.
It never reached its destination.
What do you think happened?

# The mystery

A

## A    Who was the youngest person aboard the *Mary Celeste*?

The name given to the ship when it was built in 1861 was *The Amazon*. Bad luck seemed to be with *The Amazon* from the start. During its first voyage in 1862 it was badly damaged. Then, while it was being repaired, the ship caught fire. Many similar accidents followed in the next several years. Finally *The Amazon* was sold
5 and its name was changed to *Mary Celeste*.

The owners had difficulty finding men to sail on the newly-named ship because, the sailors said, it was unlucky. In the end, however, enough sailors were found to make up a crew. The master of the ship was Benjamin Briggs, an experienced captain.
10 On its first voyage as the *Mary Celeste*, in addition to an eight-man crew, the ship carried two passengers: the captain's wife Sarah and their two-year-old daughter Sophia. On the morning of 4 November, 1872, with a cargo of 1700 barrels of crude alcohol, it left New York and headed for Genoa, Italy. The weather that day was perfect.
15 Up to the time the *Mary Celeste* reached the Azores the trip was uneventful. Once past the Azores, however, the weather changed. Captain Briggs recorded in his logbook that there was a heavy wind storm, although it was not strong enough to alarm such an experienced sailor as Briggs. On 25 November only the weather conditions and the ship's course across the Atlantic were written down in the log,
20 nothing more. That was the last entry ever made.

## B    How many people were aboard the *Mary Celeste* when the *Dei Gratia* discovered it?

Ten days later, on 5 December, Captain Morehouse of the *Dei Gratia*, another ship sailing to Europe, observed a dark spot on the horizon. They soon saw that it was a ship but something about it was rather strange.

When the *Dei Gratia* came near enough, Captain Morehouse began to study the
25 other ship through his telescope. He saw immediately that no one was steering the ship. In fact, he saw no signs of life at all!

Morehouse sent three men to discover what was wrong. As they approached the other ship the sailors were able to make out the name painted on the side: *Mary Celeste*. They realised immediately that the ship was deserted. There were no signs
30 of any kind of violence aboard, however. They noticed, too, that the ship's one lifeboat was gone.

What they found below decks was even more mystifying. In the captain's cabin everything was in perfect order. On the captain's table was a breakfast tray, with the top of a boiled egg cut off, as though someone was about to eat it. The crew's
35 section of the ship was equally in order.

The three sailors hurried back to their own ship to report to Captain Morehouse. He quickly came to the conclusion that the eleven people aboard the *Mary Celeste* had abandoned ship in a storm. The three sailors doubted this was the reason because, they said, they had seen no evidence of a storm. The captain then thought that perhaps there had been a mutiny. If that was true, said the sailors, why would the mutineers leave the ship with their captives? Other suggestions were made but all of them were unconvincing. The mystery grew.

## C      What was the most mystifying thing about the abandoned ship?

Something had to be done with the deserted ship. Captain Morehouse ordered the three sailors to sail it to nearby Gibraltar. The *Dei Gratia* went ahead and was already there when they arrived.

At Gibraltar the British authorities took charge of the *Mary Celeste* and ordered a public enquiry. They questioned Captain Morehouse and his crew closely.

Was it possible, they asked, that pirates had taken over the ship? If so, where were they? Nine barrels of the alcohol were empty. Had the crew been drinking this crude alcohol and gone crazy? Perhaps they had forced everyone aboard to jump into the sea and then, in their madness, jumped in themselves. What about the missing lifeboat? Where was it? Had Captain Briggs, for some reason, ordered everyone to abandon ship? If so, why? None of the British investigators' questions found easy answers.

What mystified them more than anything was the fact that the *Mary Celeste* had been able to remain on course for ten days without anyone to steer it. The investigators decided that possibly someone had remained on board, steering the ship, after Captain Briggs made his final log entry on 25 November. If so, who was it and where was that person now?

On 10 March, 1873, the case of the *Mary Celeste* was officially closed. The missing lifeboat had not turned up anywhere. The eleven people who had supposedly been in it were never found.

## D      What finally happened to the *Mary Celeste*?

Although the case was officially closed, interest in the *Mary Celeste* did not let up. People continued to talk about what might have happened. As late as 1913, forty years afterwards, explanations were still being given. One extraordinary explanation came in the form of a document discovered that year. It was written by a man named Abel Fosdyk, now dead, and revealed what he insisted had really happened.

According to Fosdyk, he had been an unregistered passenger on the *Mary Celeste*. During the voyage, he said, Captain Briggs ordered the ship's carpenter to construct a platform at the back of the ship for little Sophia to play on. For that purpose the carpenter had turned a big table upside down and fastened it to the deck. One morning the captain had an argument with the first mate about a man's ability to swim with his clothes on. To prove his point he jumped fully clothed into the sea and began to swim. The others aboard ship, in order to get a good view, climbed onto Sophia's platform. The weight of so many people caused the platform to collapse; they were all thrown into the sea. Sharks suddenly appeared and killed everyone except Fosdyk. He was somehow able to hold onto the remains of the collapsed platform and escape from the sharks. Eventually he was washed up on the shore somewhere in Africa.

Fosdyk's story was considered to be too fantastic and left many questions unanswered. For one thing, why had he kept silent all these years? That in itself was a mystery.

During the next eleven years the *Mary Celeste* was sold seventeen times. Finally, after 23 years of unfortunate existence, it was wrecked on some rocks in the Caribbean Sea. There it remained, slowly falling to pieces and thus ending its unglorious life in an equally unglorious way.

# Comprehension check

Some of these statements about the *Mary Celeste* are true, other are false. Decide whether each statement is true or false and correct the false ones.

1  In 1861 a ship named *The Amazon* was built; later its name was changed to *Mary Celeste*.
2  The *Mary Celeste's* cargo was 1700 barrels of crude alcohol.
3  The weather between New York and the Azores was stormy.
4  Captain Morehouse was master of the *Dei Gratia*.
5  Everything aboard the *Mary Celeste* was in perfect order.
6  Captain Morehouse's men sailed the *Mary Celeste* to the Azores.
7  British investigators thought maybe pirates had captured the people on the *Mary Celeste*.
8  After the case was officially closed in 1873 the public forgot all about the *Mary Celeste*.
9  According to Fosdyk the people aboard the *Mary Celeste* were killed by sharks.
10 During the last seventeen years of its life the *Mary Celeste* was sold eleven times.

# Language practice

## 1  Vocabulary

Here is some vocabulary from the text. You can deduce the meanings of these words from their context in the reading. In the left-hand column are the words from the reading; on the right are their definitions. Match the words with the definitions. The first one has been done for you.

| | | | | | |
|---|---|---|---|---|---|
| 1 | voyage (*l. 2*) | **k** | a | large fish that attack people |
| 2 | crew (*l. 8*) | | b | on a ship, train, plane |
| 3 | logbook (*l. 17*) | | c | went away from, left |
| 4 | steering (*l. 25*) | | d | rebellion of sailors on a ship |
| 5 | deserted (*l. 29*) | | e | workers on a ship |
| 6 | aboard (*l. 30*) | | f | guiding a ship, car, etc. |
| 7 | below decks (*l. 32*) | | g | ship's officer, second to captain |
| 8 | abandoned (*l. 38*) | | h | record of a ship's voyage |
| 9 | mutiny (*l. 40*) | | i | without people |
| 10 | first mate (*l. 73*) | | j | lower floors of a ship |
| 11 | sharks (*l. 77*) | | k | sea journey |

## 2 Phrasal verbs

These phrasal verbs also come from the text. Match them with their definitions.

| | | | |
|---|---|---|---|
| 1 | make up (*l. 8*) | a | be able to see something |
| 2 | make out (*l. 28*) | b | get control of |
| 3 | take over (*l. 48*) | c | be brought to shore |
| 4 | turn up (*l. 61*) | d | stop |
| 5 | let up (*l. 63*) | e | form |
| 6 | wash up (*l. 79*) | f | appear, be found |

## 3 Grammar: the past perfect tense of verbs

*Capt Morehouse came to the conclusion that the eleven people aboard had abandoned ship in a storm.*

The past perfect tense of verbs is formed by *had* plus a past participle (*had talked, had said*, etc.) and expresses an event that took place before another event in the past, often expressed by the simple past.

### Exercise
Complete the following sentences using the information in brackets, for example:
Captain Morehouse believed that (people aboard/abandon/ship)
*the people aboard had abandoned ship.*

1 One investigator believed that (crew/drink/too much/alcohol) _____
_____ .

2 With no one aboard, the *Mary Celeste* (able/continue/course) _____
_____ .

3 The investigators decided that (someone/remain/on board) _____
_____ .

4 Captain Briggs (jump fully clothed/into/water) _____ .

5 Everyone (climb onto/platform/watch/captain) _____ .

6 Sharks (kill/everyone/except Fosdyk) _____ .

# Discussion

Your teacher will give you instructions on how to do this part of the lesson.

# Writing

Pretend you are Abel Fosdyk writing the document that tells what, according to you, really happened aboard the *Mary Celeste* in November, 1872.

# 4. STONEHENGE :
## what was its purpose ?

On Salisbury Plain in Wiltshire, England,
there is a circle of enormous stones
that was already ancient when man began recording history
in the twelfth century.
What are these stones?
Who put them there?
How did they do it?
Most important, why?

# The mystery

## How much of the information available on Stonehenge is reliable?

No ancient monument, except perhaps the Great Pyramid of Egypt, has been the subject of as much speculation as England's Stonehenge. It is such an amazing structure that people come from all over the world to see it.

In the early 1300s British historians began writing down everything they could learn about their land and people. Of course they included the curious collection of big stones located on the plain near the town of Salisbury. Even in the twelfth century Stonehenge was already so old that information about it was vague. There is even doubt about the meaning of its name. One early historian said Stonehenge meant 'hanging stones' because they seem to hang in the air. He referred to the horizontal stones placed on top of the vertical ones.

There are many theories about Stonehenge but everything is doubtful; nothing is sure. One writer has said, 'We don't know how it was built nor why and we probably never will know.'

B
## How did the bluestones get from Wales to Salisbury Plain?

There were three phases in the construction of the monument. Archaeologists refer to them as Stonehenge I, II and III. All dates are approximate.

The first Stonehenge was constructed over a period of 700 years, beginning about 2800 BC and finishing about 2100 BC. During that time the following parts were created: a circular ditch, 300 feet in diameter; a six-foot-high bank; the 'Heel Stone', a big block of stone just outside the ditch; the 'Aubrey Holes', 56 sacred holes in the earth named after John Aubrey, who discovered them in the seventeenth century. It is believed that people of the New Stone Age were responsible for this initial phase.

Stonehenge II was worked on between 2100 BC and 2000 BC. It consisted of: a double circle of 82 bluestones, brought from the Prescelly Hills in Wales, 215 miles away – probably on rafts down the rivers (the wheel was not yet known); a wide entrance way to the monument, now called 'the Avenue'; the Heel Stone ditch. The Beaker people (called this because of a type of pottery they made) worked on the second phase. This was towards the end of the New Stone Age.

The third Stonehenge was the work of people of the Wessex Culture of the Early Bronze Age, some time between 2000 BC and 1100 BC. At that time 60 sarsen stones were put up in a circle. The meaning of sarsen is not known. These sandstone blocks were brought from an area twenty miles away; they were so heavy that they had to be transported by sledge. The circle of vertical sarsens, with a horizontal stone on top, is what people refer to as 'the true Stonehenge'.

C
## What do all authorities agree about Stonehenge?

One of the many mysteries of Stonehenge is the fact that not one of the three phases was ever completed. As a matter of fact, the Beaker people undid part of the construction done by the workers on Stonehenge I. The same was true of the Wessex people, who used some of the bluestones put up by the Beaker people for their own purposes.

The monument was under construction for nearly 2000 years. What caused these primitive people to devote so much time and energy to this astounding project that they had little time for anything else? Some archaeologists say one thing and others insist on something quite different. Everyone agrees on one point, however: Stonehenge was a kind of temple.

One belief is that this circle of stones on Salisbury Plain was a cemetery for important leaders. Human bones have been found in the Aubrey Holes, which seem to have been sacred.

Another belief is that Stonehenge was a centre of religious worship, possibly that of the Druids, who used it for their rituals. This has been a popular theory for many years, although the Druids usually worshipped in forests, not on the open plains.

| D | **Why was the cycle of eclipses important to religious leaders?** |
|---|---|

In the late eighteenth century observers noted that a person standing in the centre of Stonehenge at sunrise on 21 June, the summer solstice, and looking down the Avenue would see the sun rise above the Heel Stone, one of the oldest stones in the monument. In 1901 a British astronomer, Sir Norman Lockyer, made such a complete study of this theory that he convinced many people that the monument was actually a calendar–computer. Others have made further studies, continuing this approach.

In 1963 another astronomer, Gerald Hawkins, stated that each significant stone in the monument lined up with at least one other stone to point to some position of the sun or moon. It seems so possible that this was an accurate method of determining the length of the year that today it is the most popular theory of all. In an agricultural society this was extremely useful information to have. Also, Stonehenge may have been used to calculate the cycle of eclipses. This would be important to the religious leaders; the ability to predict such an event as an eclipse of the sun gave them great power over their people.

Today many people feel that Gerald Hawkins may have discovered the real purpose of Stonehenge. Not all archaeologists accept the Hawkins theory, however. They insist it is only a coincidence that what happens at sunrise on 21 June turns the monument into a huge calendar-computer. Perhaps one day the real truth will be known. Until then the words of the English writer, Samuel Pepys, who visited Stonehenge in the seventeenth century, persist: 'Only God knows what the stones' use was'.

## Comprehension check

Complete these sentences by choosing the correct ending for each.
1 British history began to be recorded in _____ .
   a the twelfth century AD
   b the thirteenth century AD
   c the fourteenth century AD

2 During Stonehenge II the Beaker people constructed _____ .
  a a circular ditch
  b the Heel Stone
  c the Avenue
3 Bluestones were transported from _____ .
  a Wessex
  b Salisbury Plain
  c Wales
4 Work on the third Stonehenge was done during the _____ .
  a Early Bronze Age
  b the New Stone Age
  c the Ice Age
5 The Beaker people were known for their _____ .
  a rafts
  b monuments
  c pottery
6 Everyone agrees that Stonehenge was some kind of _____ .
  a temple
  b cemetery
  c calendar

# Language practice

## 1 Vocabulary

Here is some vocabulary from the text. You can deduce the meanings of these words from their context in the reading. In the left-hand column are the words from the reading; on the right are their definitions. Match the words with the definitions. The first one has been done for you.

| | | | |
|---|---|---|---|
| 1 | plain (*l. 6*)  **c** | a | place of religious worship |
| 2 | phases (*l. 14*) | b | dishes made from baked earth |
| 3 | archaeologists (*l. 14*) | c | flat, low land |
| 4 | ditch (*l. 18*) | d | prayed to their gods |
| 5 | bank (*l. 18*) | e | periods of development |
| 6 | rafts (*l. 25*) | f | flat, wooden form used to carry things over land |
| 7 | pottery (*l. 27*) | | |
| 8 | sledge (*l. 33*) | g | some earth raised above ground level |
| 9 | temple (*l. 44*) | h | long, narrow cut in the earth; often used for water |
| 10 | worshipped (*l. 50*) | | |
| 11 | summer solstice (*l. 53*) | i | pieces of wood joined to make simple, flat boats |
| 12 | eclipse (*l. 64*) | | |
| | | j | people who study ancient monuments |
| | | k | loss of sunlight when the moon comes between the sun and the earth |
| | | l | 21 June, when sun is farthest from the equator |

## 2 Phrasal verbs

These phrasal verbs also come from the text. Match them with their definitions.

| | | | |
|---|---|---|---|
| 1 | name after (*l. 20*) | a | change a thing to something else |
| 2 | put up (*l. 31*) | b | arrange things in a row |
| 3 | line up (*l. 60*) | c | erected |
| 4 | turn into (*l. 70*) | d | give something the name of the person who discovered it |

## 3 Grammar: such a, an/so . . . that

*Stonehenge is such an amazing structure that people come from all over the world to see it. Even in the twelfth century, Stonehenge was already so old that information about it was vague. (The structure is so many centuries old that no one can imagine what its true age is.)*

Both *such a, an . . .* and *so . . . that* are patterns used with clauses expressing a result.
*Such a, an . . .* is used before a noun + *that.*
*So . . .* is used before an adjective or adverb + *that,* or the words *many, few, much, little +* noun + *that.*

### Exercise

Complete the following sentences by filling the gaps with *such* or *so.*

1 The bluestones were _____ heavy that they had to be carried to Stonehenge on rafts.
2 There are _____ many theories about the monument that we don't know what to believe.
3 It is _____ a big structure that it can be seen from many miles away.
4 Stonehenge was built _____ a long time ago that the wheel was still unknown.
5 _____ a great number of people said the Druids built Stonehenge that this was a popular belief for many years.
6 The sarsen stones weighed _____ many tons that hundreds of men were needed to put them up.
7 Stonehenge took _____ a long time to construct that no phase was ever completed.
8 Some theories of Stonehenge are _____ fantastic that it is hard to believe them.

# Discussion

Your teacher will give you instructions on how to do this part of the lesson.

# Writing

It is sunrise, 21 June, this year. You are at Stonehenge. Describe in a short paragraph what you see.

# 5. UNIDENTIFIED FLYING OBJECTS (UFOs) :

## are there such things

Have you or someone you know
ever seen an Unidentified Flying Object (UFO)?
Do you believe that creatures from outer space
are visiting our planet?
If so, what do they want?

# The mystery

## A  Are sightings of UFOs a recent thing?

On 1 January, 1254, some monks at St Albans, in England, stared up into the sky, unable to believe what they were seeing: 'a kind of large ship, elegantly shaped and of marvellous colour.'

In Basle, Switzerland, in 1566, a great number of bright, shining discs suddenly filled the night sky.

In 1897, in the United States, from California east to Virginia, tens of thousands of Americans watched a mysterious airship with flashing lights move across the country.

These and other incidents took place years before the Wright Brothers flew their first aeroplane in 1903.

During the Second World War, with so much aerial activity, many UFOs were seen but pilots were ordered to say nothing about them. Wartime security measures did not permit it; therefore, no information about UFOs was available to the public until peace came in 1945.

Certainly UFOs are nothing new. We are told they have been visiting our planet for at least 700 years, probably more.

## B  Why is former United States President Jimmy Carter mentioned here?

Today aircraft from outer space are popularly known as 'flying saucers'. This name was given to them in 1947 when an American pilot, as he flew his plane near Mount Rainier, Washington State, observed nine shining objects moving in formation at incredible speed. He described them to be 'like saucers skimming over water'. From that day on they have been called 'flying saucers'.

Since 1947 there have been sightings of UFOs almost annually, and in all parts of the world. Many articles and books have been written and a number of films made on the subject. Prominent world figures, including former United States President Jimmy Carter, claim to have seen flying saucers. There are others, however, who insist that UFOs are nothing but the products of vivid imaginations, mental disturbances and mass hallucination. Some others believe that UFOs are natural phenomena, such as meteorites, which people mistake for objects from outer space. Still others feel they are new, secret aircraft which are being tested.

## C  What do visitors from space seem to be interested in?

For many people the UFOs can be explained away as imagination, natural phenomena or new aircraft from our own planet. But what about claims by people who insist that they have seen these 'saucers' land and strange creatures emerge from them? And what about people who say that they have had personal contact with these aliens? Some claim even to have been taken inside a UFO and examined by these visitors from another planet.

In Montana, USA, a teenage boy claimed to have seen a tall, green-eyed creature step out of a flying saucer near his home. Later the boy agreed to take a test at a mental health centre; under hypnosis he described how three aliens had forced him to enter their spacecraft and examined him. They then let him go, saying he would forget the incident, which he did – except when hypnotised.

There have been various stories of people in South America making contact with beings from outer space. One evening two men were quietly fishing on the shore of a river, in Venezuela, when suddenly an unusual airship appeared in the sky above them. They watched it land in a field nearby. Several little men dressed all in white came out and began collecting grass, leaves and river water. Then, as quickly as they had arrived, they departed.

Another incident, this one in Brazil, was described by a farmer who said that a big disc landed on his property and three men emerged. They took samples of earth and plants from his garden. Then they made him enter their airship, where they began to give him a physical examination. He was inside the spaceship for about four hours and later was able to describe it in detail. Just as he was sure the creatures were going to kill him they allowed him to leave. A team of Brazilian doctors looked him over from head to foot and declared him to be in excellent physical and mental health.

## D The public seems to have lost interest in UFOs. Why?

There are many theories about what these visits by beings from other planets signify. For many people they are nothing but the products of the imaginations of unbalanced individuals. Those who do believe in the existence of UFOs, however, have a variety of ideas about them. One man, back in 1936, insisted that the visitors were friendly creatures who have been coming to our earth for centuries. Their visits, he said, have been more frequent in recent years because of the development of atomic weapons; they are afraid we will not only do away with ourselves but will be a threat to their planets as well.

Interest in UFOs rises and falls. In 1966 the US Air Force authorised a group of scientists, the Condon Committee, to make an investigation. Three years later the Committee presented a report which analysed 91 UFO cases. Two-thirds of these cases were identified as known objects, natural phenomena or products of imagination. For one-third of the cases, however, no explanation could be given; the Committee said that not enough information was available to make definite conclusions.

Since 1969 the public seems to have become bored with the subject of UFOs. This is not because it accepts the Condon report as conclusive but because there have been no sensational new sightings recently.

Who can say what may happen tomorrow? Perhaps there will be more fascinating sightings and public interest will rise once again. According to one writer, flying saucers have become a part of our general culture and people are more inclined to believe in them than not. Astronaut Ed Mitchell, the sixth man to walk on the moon, commented, 'I am convinced that some UFO sightings are real. The question is not about whether UFOs exist or not but what they are.'

# Comprehension check

Some of these statements from the text are true; others are false. Decide whether each statement is true or false, and correct the false ones.

1 Some monks in Switzerland, in 1254, saw a bright shining disc in the sky.
2 Many UFOs were seen during World War II but not reported at that time.
3 The name 'flying saucer' was created by an American pilot during World War II.
4 Some people believe UFOs are meteorites.
5 A boy in Montana was hypnotised by a tall, green-eyed creature.
6 In Venezuela two men saw aliens fishing in the river.
7 The public has, for the moment, lost interest in UFOs.
8 Ed Mitchell, the astronaut, says that he believes some UFO sightings are real.

# Language practice

## 1 Vocabulary

Here is some vocabulary from the text. You can deduce the meanings of these words from their context in the reading. In the left-hand column are the words from the reading; on the right are their definitions. Match the words with their definitions. The first one has been done for you.

| | | | | |
|---|---|---|---|---|
| 1 | monks (*l. 1*)  **j** | a | referring to things in the air |
| 2 | aerial (*l. 11*) | b | unnatural happenings |
| 3 | aircraft (*l. 17*) | c | running over the surface |
| 4 | skimming (*l. 20*) | d | come out of |
| 5 | sightings (*l. 22*) | e | beings from another place/planet |
| 6 | phenomena (*l. 28*) | f | possible danger |
| 7 | meteorites (*l. 28*) | g | flying vehicles |
| 8 | emerge (*l. 33*) | h | rocks falling from space to the earth |
| 9 | aliens (*l. 35*) | i | occasions on which something is seen |
| 10 | threat (*l. 63*) | j | group of religious men living and working together |

## 2 Phrasal verbs

These phrasal verbs also come from the text. Match them with their definitions.

| | | | |
|---|---|---|---|
| 1 | mistake for (*l. 28*) | a | remove objection with convincing information |
| 2 | explain away (*l. 31*) | | |
| 3 | look over (*l. 54*) | b | kill |
| 4 | do away with (*l. 62*) | c | examine someone/something |
| | | d | confuse somebody/something with somebody/something else |

3 **Grammar**: verbs followed by infinitive with/without *to*

Certain verbs when followed by an infinitive include *to*; others do not.

*The boy agreed to take a test.*

Some of the verbs followed by the infinitive with *to* are: *begin, want, decide, plan, like, need, agree, forget, try, love, fail, intend, expect, offer.*

*The boy described how three aliens had forced him to enter their spacecraft.*

Some verbs are followed by an *object* plus an infinitive: *want, like, love, need, ask, force, expect, permit, get, urge, invite, persuade, tell.*

*They watched the flying saucer land in a field nearby.*

Verbs followed by an infinitive without *to* always have a subject of the infinitive. Some of these verbs are: *see, observe, let, have, hear, watch, make.*

### Exercise

Complete these sentences by choosing the correct form.

1 I saw a UFO _____ over our house.    *a* fly    *b* to fly
2 A newspaper editor asked me _____ an article about it.
   *a* write    *b* to write
3 A reporter let me _____ his typewriter.    *a* use    *b* to use
4 I intended _____ the article before lunch but it wasn't possible.
   *a* finish    *b* to finish
5 I needed _____ my time and write it well.    *a* take    *b* to take
6 I wanted _____ a good job.    *a* do    *b* to do
7 I heard the editor _____ one of the reporters to read my article.
   *a* tell    *b* to tell
8 When I finished it he invited me _____ lunch with him.
   *a* have    *b* to have

# Discussion

Your teacher will give you instructions on how to do this part of the lesson.

# Writing

It is your custom to keep a diary of your activities and you write in it faithfully every day. Today you saw a flying saucer. Record it in your diary with a description of what you saw.

# 6. THE ABOMINABLE SNOWMAN :
## man or animal

The people of Nepal and Tibet
say that something they call the *Yeti*
lives in the Himalayan Mountains.
Europeans call it the *Abominable Snowman*.
In western Canada there is a
similar creature called *Sasquatch*,
and on the Pacific Coast of the United States,
*Bigfoot* inhabits the Cascade Mountains.
Are these creatures imaginary
or do they really exist?
If they do, what are they?

# The mystery

A

## In what ways are the Yeti, Sasquatch and Bigfoot alike?

'It was quite tall and looked something like a man,' said the frightened girl; then she added, 'but not completely like a man.' The people of the little town in the mountains of Nepal listened carefully to the girl describing the 'thing' that had attacked her cows that afternoon as she was bringing them home from the pasture. 'It was covered with reddish-brown hair and had a large mouth with white teeth like a human's. Its fingers were thick, with very long fingernails. Its feet were like a man's feet, but they were very large and covered with hair.' The villagers nodded to each other and said, 'The Yeti.'

Albert Ostmann, on a camping trip in western Canada, had placed his sleeping bag out under the stars and, being very tired, crawled in and dropped off almost immediately. A short while later he woke to realise that someone – or something – was carrying him through the woods. He tried to get free but it was useless; whatever was carrying him was extremely strong. Some hours later the creature stopped and put him down. The 'thing' was about eight feet tall and covered with hair. Although it was night there was enough moonlight for Albert to see it quite well. Soon others like it appeared out of the woods. They all showed great interest in Albert, touching him and making strange sounds to each other. A few days later Albert was able to get away. He was convinced that he had been a captive of Sasquatch, a man-like creature that is believed to inhabit the mountains of western Canada.

One morning in October, 1958, a construction worker near Bluff Creek, California, turned from his work and found himself looking into the eyes of a strange being covered with hair. It apparently had no wish to harm the worker but was very curious and followed him wherever he went. The man finally got rid of the creature by giving it a big piece of chocolate. In western United States this relative of Canada's Sasquatch and Nepal's Yeti is called Bigfoot because he leaves a footprint in the snow about fourteen inches long.

B

## How many Abominable Snowmen have been captured?

The local names for this strange being are different but the descriptions are quite similar. It does not look enough like a man to be called human, but it is not completely animal either. It is taller than a man – about eight feet tall – and it is covered with reddish-brown hair; it walks upright, as a man does. Its head is long, rather cone-shaped, with facial features that are half human, half ape-like. Early explorers in the Himalayas referred to it as 'one of the wild, hairy men who live in the snow.'

But is it a 'wild, hairy man' or is it an animal? Is it a bear, walking on its hind legs? Could it be some kind of ape? Or is it, perhaps, a completely unknown species? All this, of course, assuming that the Abominable Snowman exists at all.

There are too many stories about people who say they have seen one of these beings, or at least its huge footprints, to dismiss it as pure imagination. At the same time, no one has ever been able to bring one back to civilisation. In 1973 a Canadian newspaper offered $100,000 to anyone who could capture a Sasquatch alive. So far no one has come forward to collect the reward.

## C — How did this 'wild, hairy man' get the name of Abominable Snowman?

The people of Tibet have known about the Yeti for centuries, but not until 1832 was its existence reported to the West. At that time an Englishman, BH Hudson, who was living in Nepal, wrote about the 'ape-like creature'. His description, however, was not good enough to convince westerners. They said Hudson was letting his imagination run away with him. What he saw, they said, was a monkey or a Himalayan red bear.

In 1887 a British doctor connected to the Indian Army Medical Corps reported seeing quite large, human-like footprints in Sikkim. Then, in the 1920s, a period of great enthusiasm for mountaineering, explorers brought home details of Yetis in the Himalayas. They referred to them as *Abominable Snowmen*. This was an incorrect translation of *Metch Kangmi*, the Tibetan name, which really means 'disgusting snowman'. A western newspaper reporter used *Abominable Snowman* in an article and the name caught on.

Until 1921, when members of a British expedition on Mount Everest ran into a group of strange creatures, most of the reports about the Yeti had come from the natives. Colonel Howard-Bury, leader of the expedition, was rather sceptical when he saw the unusual footprints in the snow but finally declared they were marks made by the feet of wolves.

## D — How did the early settlers of western America learn about Sasquatch and Bigfoot?

Some of the remote monasteries in Tibet possess Yeti relics, such as a dried scalp or a finger, but scientists refuse to accept them as sufficient evidence until they can be removed from the monasteries for examination in a laboratory. Until now the scientists have not been permitted to take them.

There are many anecdotes about people who have seen these strange individuals, or at least their footprints, in Nepal, Tibet, Canada and the United States. Perhaps they have seen some big animal, such as a bear, walking upright like a man. Maybe the footprints they saw were animal tracks that had been distorted by the heat of the sun on the snow. To the natives of Nepal the Yetis are supernatural beings and for that reason are placed in the same category as witches and ghosts. Legends about them have been part of the folkore of Himalayan villages for centuries. As far as North America is concerned, the Indians told early settlers of the West enough stories about big, hairy men living in the mountains to put them on the alert.

Do such creatures really exist? If so, are they men or animals, and if animals, what kind? Could they be a species completely unknown to us? Perhaps one day an Abominable Snowman will be captured and examined by scientists. Then we'll know.

# Comprehension check

Complete these sentences by filling the gap with the correct word.

1 Albert Ostmann was on a _____ trip in Canada.
   *a* business    *b* camping    *c* fishing

2 The Yeti has a long, _____ head.
   *a* human    *b* ape-like    *c* cone-shaped

3 The construction worker in California gave Bigfoot some _____ .
   *a* chocolate    *b* money    *c* bread

4 In _____ some mountain climbers saw a group of Yetis on Mount Everest.
   *a* 1832    *b* 1921    *c* 1887

5 *Metch Kangmi*, a Tibetan name, means _____ .
   *a* explorer    *b* European snowman    *c* disgusting snowman

6 Until 1921, most reports about the Yeti had come from _____ .
   *a* explorers    *b* natives    *c* wolves

7 Yeti relics can be found in _____ .
   *a* monasteries    *b* laboratories    *c* museums

8 The Nepalese belief in Yetis places them in the same category as _____ .
   *a* humans    *b* ghosts    *c* animals

# Language practice

## 1 Vocabulary

Here is some vocabulary from the text. You can deduce the meanings of these words from their context in the reading. In the left-hand column are the words from the reading; on the right are their definitions. Match the words with the definitions. The first one has been done for you.

| | | | |
|---|---|---|---|
| 1 | nodded (*l. 7*) **e** | a | changed slightly |
| 2 | upright (*l. 31*) | b | skin of the head |
| 3 | cone-shaped (*l. 32*) | c | people living in a newly-developed place |
| 4 | features (*l. 32*) | d | parts of the face, eg eyes |
| 5 | hind (*l. 35*) | e | moved the head forward and back as sign of agreement |
| 6 | species (*l. 37*) | | |
| 7 | reward (*l. 43*) | f | back, rear (of an animal) |
| 8 | relics (*l. 62*) | g | round at the bottom, narrow at the top |
| 9 | scalp (*l. 62*) | h | group of beings with similar characteristics |
| 10 | anecdotes (*l. 66*) | i | standing on back legs |
| 11 | distorted (*l. 70*) | j | remains of someone, often in a religious context |
| 12 | settlers (*l. 74*) | k | stories |
| | | l | money offered for information or finding someone/something |

## 2 Phrasal verbs

These phrasal verbs also come from the text. Match them with their definitions.

| | | | |
|---|---|---|---|
| 1 | drop off (*l. 10*) | a | become popular |
| 2 | get away (*l. 18*) | b | present oneself |
| 3 | get rid of (*l. 24*) | c | meet unexpectedly |
| 4 | come forward (*l. 43*) | d | make someone/something leave |
| 5 | run away with (*l. 48*) | e | allow someone/something to take |
| 6 | catch on (*l. 56*) | | control (eg imagination) |
| 7 | run into (*l. 57*) | f | go to sleep |
| | | g | escape |

## 3 Grammar: *very, quite, rather, enough*

*Alex*:     That film about the Abominable Snowman was *very* good. What did you think, Tom?

*Tom*:     I don't usually like that kind of movie but I thought this one was *rather* good. Did you like it, Helen?

*Helen*:   I thought it was *quite* good, but not fantastic.

*Alex*:     Well, I thought it was good *enough* to see again!

The adverbs *very, quite, rather* are used to intensify (ie make stronger) an adjective or another adverb, which they precede. The difference between them is one of degree of intensity in meaning. *Very* is the strongest, meaning *much*; *quite* and *rather* are similar, both being less strong than *very*. The intensity of both *quite* and *rather* can be changed by intonation.

*Enough* can be either an adjective or an adverb. It means *as much/many as needed*; as an adjective it precedes the noun it modifies (eg *I haven't got enough money*); as an adverb if follows the adjective it modifies (eg *She's not old enough*).

### Exercise

Answer these questions using *very, quite, rather* or *enough*.

1 Do you think Albert Ostmann was frightened when the Sasquatch carried him away?
2 In your opinion, is Bigfoot ugly?
3 Is the Abominable Snowman timid, do you think?
4 How sceptical are scientists about the Yeti, Sasquatch and Bigfoot?
5 Is *Abominable Snowman* a good translation of *Metch Kangmi*?
6 How would feel if you were in Nepal and saw a Yeti?

# Discussion

Your teacher will give you instructions on how to do this part of the lesson.

# Writing

You have just returned from a holiday in the Cascade Mountains in Washington State, USA, where you saw Bigfoot. Your local newspaper has asked you to write a short article about your experience.

# 7. LIZZIE BORDEN :

## did she murder her parents

On Thursday, 4 August, 1892,
Andrew Borden and his wife were found dead
in their home in the quiet, provincial mill town of
Fall River, Massachusetts, USA.
Some people said their daughter Lizzie had murdered them.
Others believed it was someone else.
Was it Lizzie?
Or could it have been someone else?
What do you think?

# The mystery

A

## What was one of the reasons Lizzie hated her stepmother?

At 8.00 am, 4 August, the day was already the hottest of the year. In the dining room of their big white house on Second Street, members of the Borden family were having breakfast. At the table sat prominent 70-year-old businessman Andrew Borden, his second wife, Abby and a brother-in-law of Andrew's, John Morse. John was manager of one of the Borden farms. Andrew's two daughters by his first marriage, Emma and Lizzie, were absent. Emma was visiting friends in a nearby town.

Lizzie, a rather unattractive, inhibited, unmarried woman of 32 had not yet come downstairs. Except for her hobby, fishing, and her participation in church activities, Lizzie spent a lot of time alone, often up in her room. About every four months she had what her family called 'funny turns'. At such times she did peculiar, inexplicable things; she never remembered these incidents afterwards. We now realise that her 'funny turns' were attacks of epilepsy.

Lizzie disliked her stepmother intensely, especially after Andrew signed some property over to his wife's sister that his daughters felt should be theirs.

Andrew Borden was a person who enjoyed making money but hated spending it. When his daughters asked him for money he almost always turned them down. The Bordens were rich but they certainly did not live like people with money. Andrew also had the reputation in Fall River of being a very hard man in business dealings; as a result, he had many enemies.

## B

## Why did the Bordens keep their doors locked?

There was one other person in the house that torrid August morning: Bridget, the Irish maid. Bridget was in the kitchen preparing to go outside and wash the windows. She was quite unhappy about it. She did not feel well and resented Mrs Borden's orders to wash the windows. Bridget was not the only one who felt ill. With the exception of Lizzie, everyone in the house had stomach trouble. They decided it was something they had eaten the night before.

The time was now 8.45 am John Morse left the house to visit other relatives in Fall River. Andrew also departed, heading for the financial district.

Lizzie descended the stairs just as her father was going out of the front door. She greeted Bridget but said nothing to her stepmother. Abby climbed the stairs to the second floor bedrooms to make the beds. Bridget went outside to wash the windows. She took the key to the kitchen door with her. Since a robbery two months before the Bordens were extremely cautious about locking their doors. Lizzie began ironing some clothes. It was now 9.30 am.

## C

## According to Lizzie, where was she when her father was killed?

At 10.40 someone knocked at the front door. Bridget, now working inside the house, hurried to see who it was. She heard someone laugh behind her as she struggled with the key. It was Lizzie, standing on the stairs. At last the maid got the door open. The person on the other side was Andrew Borden; he had forgotten his keys.

As Bridget returned to the kitchen, Lizzie came down to the sitting room and told her father, 'Your wife has gone out. She had a note from someone who was sick.' Andrew said that he, too, felt rather weak and decided to stretch out on the sofa and take a nap before lunch. 40

Lizzie went back to her ironing. Bridget, who had finished washing the windows inside and out, said she still felt ill. Lizzie told her to go up to her room and rest until it was time to make lunch. As the girl climbed to her small, hot, third-floor room, she heard the clock strike 11.00. 45

Ten minutes later Lizzie called out from downstairs: 'Bridget! Come quick! Father's dead. Somebody came in and killed him!'

The astonished maid rushed down the stairs and found Lizzie standing by the kitchen door. 'Go across the street and get Dr Bowen,' she said. 'Run!' 50

## D Where was Abby Borden?

When the doctor arrived, Lizzie explained, 'Just as I was returning to the house from the barn I heard a loud groan. The kitchen door was wide open.'

The doctor quickly examined Andrew's body and discovered that the man had been struck in the head eleven times with an axe. Being asleep, he never knew what hit him. 55

Lizzie told Bridget to go to ask her friend Alice Russell to come and stay with her. Meanwhile, another neighbour, Adelaide Churchill, had seen Dr Bowen enter the house next door and rushed over to find out what had happened. When she asked where Abby was, Lizzie replied that she did not know. Then she added, 'But I believe I heard her come in a short while ago.' She turned to Bridget, 'Go upstairs and see.' 60

Mrs Churchill accompanied the Irish girl. They found Abby Borden lying face down on the guest room floor. She had been hit on the back of the head nineteen times with an axe. 65

It was now 11.40, half an hour after Andrew Borden's bloody, lifeless body had been discovered in the sitting room. Policemen were already surrounding the house and a crowd of curious people had gathered in the street. The news had travelled fast.

## E Why did Lizzie want to buy poison?

About this time John Morse returned from his visit across town. He did a very strange thing when he saw the crowd in the street: he went round to the back of the house and began eating pears from one of the trees. As soon as he was told what had happened, however, he went into the house. He explained where he had been to the police, but they were not fully convinced. For one thing, his manner was too casual. 70
75

The police made a complete search of the house but found nothing suspicious. Nor did they find a note asking Mrs Borden to go to a sick friend. Later someone reported that a stranger had been seen near the house earlier that morning; he was never seen again.

Lizzie was able to account for every move she had made that morning; however, the police considered her to be their number one suspect. Lizzie's calm cool manner under the horrible circumstances caused them to be suspicious. In addition, she kept contradicting herself.

There was another matter that caused the police to suspect Lizzie. The day before the murder she had gone to several shops trying to buy prussic acid, a deadly poison. She wanted it, she said, to kill moths in her fur coat. The shop owners refused to sell it to her.

According to Lizzie, she had been in the house all morning, except when, shortly after her father's return home, she went to the barn to get some things she needed for a fishing trip. Then, when she returned to the house, she discovered her father's body.

## F — How long did it take the jury to reach a verdict?

One week later Lizzie was arrested. There was, however, no real evidence against her. What motive did she have? She hated her stepmother, it is true, but not enough to kill her. She adored her father, so why would she kill him? For his money? She and her sister Emma would become rich the moment he died. What about Bridget, the maid, and John Morse, Andrew's brother-in-law? Couldn't one of them have committed the murder?

The trial began on 5 June, 1892, and lasted ten days. At first the public and press were anti-Lizzie Borden, but little by little they came round. How could a quiet, respectable, mature woman like Lizzie commit such a horrible crime?

Finally the jury left the courtroom but was out only one hour. When they returned they delivered a verdict of not guilty. The courtroom suddenly became wild with cheers and applause.

Once more life in Fall River became normal. The two Borden sisters, now that they had their father's money, bought a lovely big new house in the most fashionable section of Fall River. They lived together in this beautiful, spacious mansion for several years. Then they quarrelled and Emma moved out, leaving Lizzie all by herself in the empty house. In 1927, Lizzie passed away at the age of 67, alone and unloved.

Today visitors to Fall River almost always ask to see the old Borden house on Second Street. 'Did Lizzie Borden really murder her parents?' they ask. The people of Fall River simply shake their heads and say, 'No one will ever know.' Probably not, but on the other hand, if Lizzie did not commit the murder, who did?

# Comprehension check

Look back at the reading and find the information to fill the gaps in this paragraph.

Lizzie Borden's father, a very rich man, hated _____ money. Lizzie thought that her _____, Abby, had too much influence on Andrew Borden. That was one of the reasons she _____ Abby. Once Lizzie asked her father for money to entertain some church friends but Andrew _____ her request. Lizzie became furious when her father _____ some property to Abby's sister; it was supposed to go to Lizzie and her sister, _____ . It is possible that when this happened Lizzie had one of her attacks of _____ . As a result, she may have murdered her parents with an _____ . The _____ , during the trial, brought in a _____ of not guilty, but was she really innocent? We'll never know.

# Language practice

## 1 Vocabulary

Here is some vocabulary from the text. You can deduce the meanings of these words from their context in the reading. In the left-hand column are the words from the reading; on the right are their definitions. Match the words with the definitions. The first one has been done for you.

| | | | |
|---|---|---|---|
| 1 | inhibited (*l. 8*) **b** | a | short sleep |
| 2 | stepmother (*l. 14*) | b | unable to express true feelings |
| 3 | torrid (*l. 21*) | c | sharp tool to cut wood |
| 4 | resented (*l. 23*) | d | twelve people who decide a law case in court |
| 5 | nap (*l. 43*) | | |
| 6 | barn (*l. 53*) | e | saying the opposite of something said before |
| 7 | groan (*l. 53*) | | |
| 8 | axe (*l. 55*) | f | decision made in a law case |
| 9 | contradicting (*l. 83*) | g | extremely hot |
| 10 | motive (*l. 93*) | h | deep sound made by someone in pain |
| 11 | jury (*l. 101*) | i | reason for committing a crime |
| 12 | verdict (*l. 102*) | j | later wife of one's father |
| | | k | farm building for storing things in |
| | | l | disliked someone for something he/she had done |

## 2 Phrasal verbs

These phrasal verbs also come from the text. Match them with their definitions.

| | | | |
|---|---|---|---|
| 1 | sign over (*l. 14*) | a | lie down |
| 2 | turned down (*l. 17*) | b | die |
| 3 | stretch out (*l. 42*) | c | refuse a request |
| 4 | come round (*l. 99*) | d | give rights with a formal document |
| 5 | pass away (*l. 108*) | e | agree after first refusing |

## 3 Grammar: order of adjectives before a noun

*Lizzie Borden was an unattractive, young, unmarried American woman.*

Certain rules must be observed in placing adjectives in the correct order before a noun. If there are determiners, such as *as*, *the*, *that*, *my*, etc., these will precede other adjectives. Ordinal numbers (*first*, *second*, *fifth*.) come next, followed by cardinal numbers (*one*, *seven*, *fifty*).

Then come all other adjectives. These, however, are the ones that cause problems for students. A plan for these adjectives is helpful. With very few exceptions, it is as follows:

(after 1, determiners; 2, ordinal numbers; 3, cardinal numbers)
4 quality words (of general description; they can go in any order in respect to each other)
5 size (*big*, *long*)
6 age, temperature (*old*, *hot*)
7 shape (*round*, *square*)
8 colour (*blue*, *green*)
9 participle (*spoken*, *running*)
10 origin or location (*Portuguese*, *western*);
11 material (*glass*, *metal*)
12 noun used as an adjective (*school*, as in *school teacher*).

Luckily, not all categories are likely to be included in a sentence but those that are usually follow this order, as in:

| beautiful | big | old | square | grey | repainted | French | stone | school | house |
|---|---|---|---|---|---|---|---|---|---|
| 4 | 5 | 6 | 7 | 8 | 9 | 10 | 11 | 12 | |

### Exercise
Put the adjectives in brackets in the correct order before the noun.
1 Abby Borden was a (grey-haired, round, short) woman.
2 John Morse was a (middle-aged, pleasant, tall) man.
3 Lizzie's sister Emma was a (41-year-old, quiet, thin) woman.
4 Lizzie's friend Alice was a (English, kind, little) lady.
5 George Robinson, who was Lizzie's lawyer, was a (brilliant, persuasive, likeable) man.
6 Bridget, the maid, was a (Irish, large, hard-working) girl.

# Discussion

Your teacher will give you instructions on how to do this part of the lesson.

# Writing

You are a neighbour of the Bordens, living opposite them on Second Street. It is the afternoon of 4 August, 1892. You have been asked by the local newspaper to write an article telling what you know about the crime.

# 8. THE BERMUDA TRIANGLE :

## is it a triangle of death

What have you heard
about the Bermuda Triangle?
Perhaps you know that ships and planes have been disappearing
in this part of the Atlantic Ocean for many years.
But do you know why?
Is there a logical explanation?

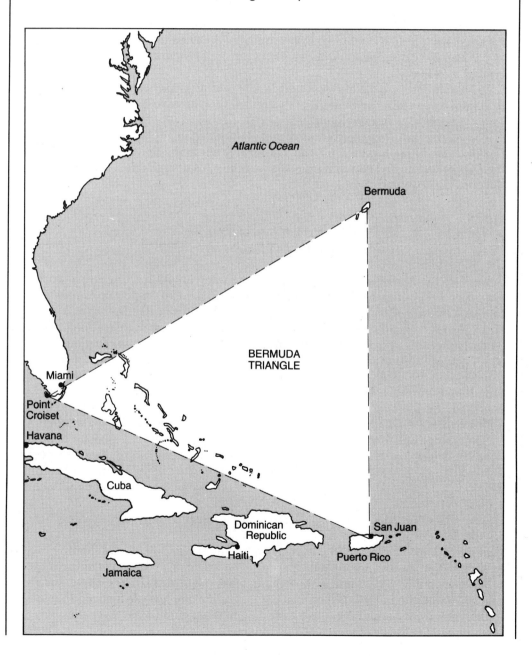

# The mystery

## What happened to the *Cyclops* and the *Deering*?

For hundreds of years weird things have been happening in that part of the Atlantic Ocean known today as the Bermuda Triangle. Until 1964 when an American writer used the term 'Bermuda Triangle' in a magazine article it was called, among other things, the Devil's Triangle, the Graveyard of the Atlantic, and the Triangle of Death.

You will see on the map (page 41) that the region in question is an almost perfect triangle, with one point Bermuda, another the east coast of Florida, and the third one Puerto Rico. Since the beginning of the twentieth century many ships and planes have disappeared there without a trace of them or without their crews ever being found.

In March 1918, a US Navy supply ship, the *Cyclops*, vanished while sailing from Barbados to Norfolk, Virginia; there were 309 men on board. No remains of the ship or its crew were ever found.

The sailing ship *Deering* was discovered abandoned near Cape Hatteras, North Carolina, on 30 January, 1921. Cape Hatteras is not in the Bermuda Triangle but the *Deering* had passed through that section of the Atlantic and it is supposed that the crew disappeared there.

**B**
## How many planes disappeared on 5 December, 1945?

Since 1945 the Bermuda Triangle has attracted the attention of the entire world. On 5 December of that year something happened that caused people everywhere to take interest in the region. It was on that day that Flight 19, a group of five US Navy planes, took off from Fort Lauderdale, Florida, on a routine training flight. The weather was perfect. For two hours everything went according to plan. Then the Naval Air Station at Fort Lauderdale began to receive unusual radio messages from Flight 19. The five planes were lost and their instruments were not functioning properly. Conversations among the pilots of the five planes seemed confused. At 4 pm, after the leader of the flight turned over the command to another pilot for no apparent reason, all communication with Flight 19 ended.

Something was definitely wrong with this group of five planes; search operations were started immediately. For several days planes flew over the area where Flight 19 had last been heard from. Then one of the search planes, a Martin Mariner, also disappeared. No trace of it or of the five planes that made up Flight 19 was ever found.

The rumours started. One was that during the final communication with Flight 19 the hysterical description of a gigantic flying saucer was heard. Another rumour claimed that one of the airmen on the flight was later found floating in a rubber life raft; he was talking wildly about a 'weird airship' that had captured the other men on Flight 19. None of the rumours was confirmed. In fact, there was no official explanation at all concerning the tragedy. Some people insisted that the authorities knew something they were not making public but that they were hushing up the incident.

## C   What caused the public to start doubting reports about the Bermuda Triangle?

After 5 December, 1945, the world became aware of the strange things happening in the 'Triangle of Death'. Reports began to appear in the newspapers and on the radio about other unusual happenings. Between 1947 and 1973 over 140 ships and planes, with more than 1000 people aboard in total, vanished, leaving no evidence to show what had happened to them. Many explanations were given; few people were convinced by them. The most acceptable theory was that UFOs were collecting human specimens to examine. For some reason the Bermuda Triangle was where they entered the earth's atmosphere to do this.

Since 1960 many articles, even full-length books, have been written about the Bermuda Triangle. For a number of years the public was fascinated and read everything available on the subject. Then, in the late 1970s, people began to grow sceptical about the various things reported; they found them too fantastic to be true.

## D   What was Kusche's final comment in his book about the Bermuda Triangle?

In 1975 a librarian, Lawrence D Kusche, who was also an experienced pilot, wrote a book entitled *The Bermuda Triangle Mystery Solved*. In preparing his book Kusche went to the original records to learn what had actually happened. Unlike other writers on the subject he was not content to depend on the legends that had been reported for many years. He discovered to his own satisfaction that there were quite logical explanations for almost every one of the Bermuda Triangle mysteries.

According to Kusche, poor judgement on the part of the leader of Flight 19 and the Fort Lauderdale Naval Air Station had caused the tragedy. When the five planes took off from Fort Lauderdale the weather had been beautiful; within a short time it changed. Thus, the flight did not disappear on a sunny day, as most people thought, but on a stormy day. In the storm the planes ran out of fuel and dropped into the sea. As far as the search plane was concerned, the Martin Mariners had exploded in the air. It was not unusual, said Kusche, for these 'flying gas tanks', as the Martin Mariners were sometimes called, to explode.

In another mysterious case the *Marine Sulphur Queen*, a large ship carrying sulphur from Beaumont, Texas, to Norfolk, Virginia, disappeared in February, 1963. It was, according to Kusche, badly designed and its cargo had been improperly loaded. Very possibly it broke up in a stormy sea and went down so quickly that there was no time even to send a radio message.

Kusche's list of cases was long but he studied each one carefully and found what he considered to be logical explanations for all of them. He concluded his book with the statement that there is a great amount of sea and air traffic in this part of the Atlantic Ocean; for that reason the number of disappearances over the years has not, in Kusche's estimation, been excessive.

Not everyone accepts Kusche's theories, however, especially those who are convinced that extraterrestrial beings are responsible for the disappearance of the missing ships and planes. In any case, the Bermuda Triangle continues to be a mystery and will probably remain so for many years to come.

# Comprehension check

Look back at the reading and find information to complete these sentences.

1 The three points of the Bermuda Triangle are _____ .
2 The *Cyclops* disappeared while sailing from _____ .
3 On 5 December, 1945, Flight 19 took off on a _____ .
4 No traces of Flight 19 were _____ .
5 Between 1947 and 1973 _____ .
6 The most popular belief about the Bermuda Triangle was _____ .
7 Lawrence D Kusche was a librarian as well as _____ .
8 Kusche studied the disappearances carefully and concluded that _____ .

# Language practice

## 1 Vocabulary

Here is some vocabulary from the text. You can deduce the meanings of these words from their context in the reading. In the left-hand column are the words from the reading; on the right are their definitions. Match the words with the definitions. The first one has been done for you.

| | | | |
|---|---|---|---|
| 1 | weird (*l. 1*) **b** | a | energy-producing material such as gas and oil |
| 2 | graveyard (*l. 4*) | b | very strange and unusual |
| 3 | trace (*l. 9*) | c | from another planet |
| 4 | remains (*l. 12*) | d | ordinary, everyday |
| 5 | routine (*l. 21*) | e | too much |
| 6 | became aware (*l. 41*) | f | something left behind after, for example, an accident |
| 7 | fuel (*l. 65*) | g | yellow strong-smelling substance used in industry and medicine |
| 8 | sulphur (*l. 70*) | h | cemetery, where the dead are buried |
| 9 | excessive (*l. 78*) | i | gained knowledge of something |
| 10 | extraterrestrial (*l. 80*) | j | evidence showing the presence of something |

## 2 Phrasal verbs

These phrasal verbs also come from the text. Match them with their definitions.

| | | | |
|---|---|---|---|
| 1 | take off (*l. 21*) | a | give control to another person |
| 2 | turn over (*l. 26*) | b | possess no more of something |
| 3 | hush up (*l. 40*) | c | sink to the bottom of the sea |
| 4 | run out of (*l. 65*) | d | keep information from the public |
| 5 | go down (*l. 72*) | e | rise into the air |

3 **Grammar**: for/since

*Ships and planes have been disappearing in this part of the Atlantic Ocean for many years.*
*Since 1945 the Bermuda Triangle has attracted the attention of the entire world.*

The word *for* introduces a phrase of duration in which the length of time is stated: *for an hour, for six weeks*.
The word *since* indicates the beginning of a period of time; the end of the period is the moment of speaking: *since 3 July, since I arrived, since John's birthday*.
Both words are often used with the present perfect tense, simple or continuous, which refers to an action begun in the past and continuing to the present.

**Exercise**
Fill in the gaps in these sentences with *for* or *since*.
1 The area has been called the Bermuda Triangle _____ 1964.
2 Strange things have occurred in that part of the Atlantic _____ the early 1900s.
3 Many ships and planes have vanished _____ that time.
4 Flight 19 had been gone _____ two hours.
5 Search planes flew over the area _____ several days.
6 _____ 1960 many books and articles have been written about the 'Triangle of Death'.
7 People have been more sceptical _____ the late 1970s.
8 The Bermuda Triangle will probably continue to be a mystery _____ many years.

# Discussion

Your teacher will give you instructions on how to do this part of the lesson.

# Writing

According to one rumour about Flight 19 a member of the crew was found floating in the water in a rubber life raft. He talked about a 'weird airship' that captured his companions and took them away. You, as a newspaper reporter, have an opportunity to talk to this man. Write your interview with him as a dialogue.

# 9.  AMBROSE BIERCE :

## what happened to him ?

Imagine that you are a famous writer.
You think that after you die
no one will remember you or your writings.
What can you do about it?

*Gregory Peck as
Ambrose Bierce in
Columbia Pictures'
OLD GRINGO*

## The mystery

A | **Why was Ambrose Bierce
called 'Bitter Bierce'?**

One of the most successful American short story writers at the turn of the century was Ambrose Bierce. In December 1913 he disappeared, never to be seen or heard from again. Because of things he said shortly before he vanished it is possible that he planned the final days of his life that way. He was afraid that once he died both
5   he and his writings would be forgotten. He did not want that to happen.
    In 1861, at the age of nineteen, Bierce found his purpose in life: the military. The Civil War between the northern and southern states broke out at that time,

and shortly afterwards Bierce joined the northern army. He loved military life and fought in many important battles. He was wounded twice, once quite seriously in the head. Bierce was never the same after this head injury; be became bitter, suspicious of people and concerned about death.

When peace came in 1865 Bierce travelled west to San Francisco. There he met and married a socially-prominent young woman, Mary Ellen Day, and became the father of two sons and a daughter. However, in 1871, because his marriage was no longer happy, he left San Francisco and went to England, settling down in London to become a writer. Two years later a collection of his stories was published. Because of his sharp tongue and the pessimistic nature of his stories, he earned the nickname of 'Bitter Bierce'.

## B  Bierce's stories were well liked but he as a person was not. Why not?

When Bierce returned to San Francisco in 1876 he was already a celebrity because of his success in England. He became a magazine editor and was soon recognised as the literary leader of the city. Unfortunately, it was also at this time he developed a severe case of asthma, which stayed with him for the rest of his life.

One of the leading newspapermen in San Francisco at that time was William Randolph Hearst. Hearst asked Bierce to write a column for his paper, *The Examiner*. Bierce accepted the position and wrote about everybody and everything, expressing his observations in his usual sarcastic manner. Because of his sarcasm he had very few friends but many enemies.

Ten years after going to work for Hearst, Ambrose Bierce was transferred to Washington, DC. He liked the capital city because, he said, the climate was good for his asthma. He remained there until 1909, at which time he retired from newspaper work to edit the stories and articles he had written over the years. His secretary, Carrie Christiansen, worked closely with him on this project. When they finished in 1912, Bierce was seventy years old. What was he going to do now?

## C  What did Bierce write to a friend in San Francisco?

In the years following the Civil War Bierce read all he could find on military matters. Because of his war experience and extensive reading, he became a military expert. He felt sure that he could secure a position as adviser to military leaders in some part of the world. That, he decided, was what he would do with the rest of his life.

Then a revolution broke out in Mexico. Pancho Villa and Venustiano Carranza were the leaders of the rebels fighting the official forces. One summer's day in 1913 Bierce told his secretary his plan: he was going to tour the Civil War battlefields; then he would go to Mexico. He carried out the first part of his plan as proposed.

From the moment he left Washington DC Bierce wrote to his secretary almost daily. He also wrote, though less frequently, to his daughter Helen. To one of his friends in San Francisco he said he wished to end his career in a more glorious way than just dying in bed. 'I've decided to go to Mexico to find a soldier's grave,' he wrote.

47

## How was Bierce's wish fulfilled?

Bierce's last letter to his secretary, dated 16 December, 1913, was from Laredo, Texas. 'I go to Mexico with a definite purpose which I cannot yet disclose,' he
50 said. He sent that letter from Laredo; the next day, as far as anyone knows, he entered Mexico.

Some people believe that Bierce never actually crossed the border, however, but went to some isolated place in the United States where he could end his days peacefully and alone, possibly a place in the mountains that would be good for his
55 asthma. Others believe he went to Europe as an adviser to the British military leader, Lord Kitchener, during World War I.

Several months passed and when no one heard from Bierce his daughter asked the US State Department to locate her father. A search was made but the only result was an unconfirmed report that Bierce had actually reached Pancho Villa's
60 headquarters. Except for two or three similar rumours, Bierce was never heard from again. Nevertheless, his wish to be remembered was fulfilled because twenty years later rumours about him were still going around. Even today the subject of what happened to Ambrose Bierce fascinates people.

## Comprehension check

Some of these statements about Ambrose Bierce are true; others are false. Decide whether each statement is true or false and correct the false ones.
1 Ambrose Bierce was a well-known novelist.
2 During the Civil War he was a soldier in the army of the north.
3 He hated army life.
4 He did not like being a husband.
5 William Randolph Hearst invited Bierce to write a column for his newspaper.
6 Bierce liked the climate of Washington DC.
7 He wanted to be a military adviser but was sure no one would want to use his services.
8 A revolution broke out in Mexico between Pancho Villa and Venustiano Carranza.
9 Bierce wrote to his secretary almost every day.
10 We know for certain that Bierce entered Mexico on 17 December, 1913.

## Language practice

### 1 Vocabulary

Here is some vocabulary from the text. You can deduce the meanings of these words from their context in the reading. In the left-hand column are the words from the reading; on the right are their definitions. Match the words with the definitions. The first one has been done for you.

| | | | |
|---|---|---|---|
| 1 | turn of the century (*l. 1*) **c** | a | hurt, injured |
| | | b | make something known/public |
| 2 | vanished (*l. 3*) | c | start of a new hundred-year period, eg 1900 |
| 3 | wounded (*l. 9*) | | |
| 4 | bitter (*l. 10*) | d | illness which affects breathing |
| 5 | pessimistic (*l. 17*) | e | happened as promised |
| 6 | celebrity (*l. 19*) | f | disappeared |
| 7 | asthma (*l. 22*) | g | sharp and cruel humour |
| 8 | sarcasm (*l. 27*) | h | someone who affects/acts against authority |
| 9 | rebel (*l. 40*) | i | always looking at the negative side |
| 10 | disclose (*l. 49*) | j | filled with resentment |
| 11 | fulfilled (*l. 61*) | k | famous person |

## 2 Phrasal verbs

These phrasal verbs also come from the text. Match them with their definitions.

| | | | |
|---|---|---|---|
| 1 | hear from (*l. 2*) | a | start suddenly (war, epidemic) |
| 2 | break out (*l. 7*) | b | receive news from someone |
| 3 | settle down (*l. 15*) | c | establish oneself in a place |
| 4 | carry out (*l. 42*) | d | circulate |
| 5 | go around (*l. 62*) | e | perform or complete |

## 3 Grammar: *because/because of*

*Bierce liked Washington DC because the climate was good for his asthma.*
*When Bierce returned to San Francisco he was already a celebrity because of his success in England.*

*Because* is followed by a clause. *Because of* is followed by a noun or noun phrase.

### Exercise
Fill in the gaps in these sentences with *because* or *because of*.
1 Bierce made many enemies _____ his sarcasm.
2 Hearst invited Bierce to do a column for his newspaper _____ he liked his style of writing.
3 _____ a head injury in the war, he became bitter and suspicious.
4 Bierce had asthma attacks each year _____ he didn't look after himself.
5 _____ his love for military life Bierce read everything he could about it.
6 Bierce said he was going to Mexico _____ he wanted to work with Pancho Villa.

## Discussion

Your teacher will give you instructions on how to do this part of the lesson.

## Writing

Pretend you are Bierce's daughter, Helen. Write a letter to the US State Department, explaining the situation and requesting help in locating your father.

49

# 10. ANASTASIA :
## was she really the Tsar's daughter

In 1918, during the Russian Revolution,
Tsar Nicholas II and members of his family
were shot by the Bolsheviks.
There were rumours, however,
that one of the daughters, Anastasia, escaped.
Some people say she did not get away
but died with the rest of the family.
Do you know anything about this mystery?

# The mystery

## Why was the mysterious woman called 'Miss Unknown'?

It was a cold winter's night – 22 February, 1920, to be exact. A policeman, walking along Berlin's Landwehr Canal, heard a loud splash and quickly jumped in and pulled out a young woman. With this event began a story that initiated the longest lawsuit in legal history.

The young woman was taken to a mental hospital. She carried no identification and refused to give her name; it was obvious that she was not used to doing anything that she did not want to do.

The people at the hospital began to call her 'Miss Unknown'. A physical examination of the young woman, who appeared to be about twenty years old, showed that her body was covered with scars. She spoke very little and when she did it was in German, although with a foreign accent. She was usually polite, sometimes even pleasant. After a time she seemed to get used to hospital life.

One of the other patients at the hospital had read an article about the Russian Tsar, Nicholas II, and his family. A photograph accompanied the article. The woman decided that the mysterious new patient looked very much like one of the Tsar's daughters. In addition, 'Miss Unknown' became depressed when she saw the photo. One day in the autumn of 1921, however, she admitted that she was the Grand Duchess Anastasia Nicholaievna of Russia.

**B**
## Why did Anastasia want to go to Berlin?

Her story came out slowly and painfully. Russia was in the middle of a revolution. The Bolsheviks had captured the Imperial family and were holding them prisoners in a house in the town of Ekaterinburg. On the evening of 16 July, 1918, the family was led to a basement room and shot. The bodies were taken out to an old mine and burned.

According to the young woman's story, she, Anastasia (as we shall now call her), fainted just as the soldiers fired their guns. Her sister Tatania fell on top of her, protecting Anastasia and thus saving her life. The next thing Anastasia remembered, she was in a farm cart being smuggled out of Russia by one of the guards at Ekaterinburg, Alexander Tschaikovsky, who was secretly loyal to the Tsar. When he saw that Anastasia was alive he took her to his family's farm. Then, with the Tschaikovskys accompanying her, Anastasia began a long, hard journey to Romania.

Finally they reached Bucharest. Anastasia remained there for a year, during which time she had Alexander Tschaikovsky's son, then married the father. Not long after that Alexander was murdered by Bolsheviks who had discovered how he had helped the Tsar's daughter to escape.

Taking her brother-in-law, Sergei Tschaikovsky, with her, Anastasia headed for Germany, leaving her son with the Tschaikovsky family. She was anxious to get to Berlin, where members of her mother's family lived.

## C > What was possibly the reason for Anastasia's bad moods?

At last she and Sergei reached Berlin. They checked in at a hotel and made plans to try to find Anastasia's grandmother the next day. The following morning, when she went to Sergei's room, Anastasia discovered that he had disappeared.

All day she walked the streets of Berlin, not knowing what to do; she was not used to being alone and making her own decisions. She had come to Berlin to find her mother's relatives but now, with nothing to identify her, she was afraid to go to them. Night fell and as she walked beside the Landwehr Canal she became so discouraged that she jumped into the water.

Later, when members of the Russian colony read an article about 'Anastasia' in the newspapers some of them came to the hospital to see her. A few were convinced that yes, she was the daughter of the Tsar. Others, however, called her an imposter.

When the young woman became well enough she was invited to go to live with Baron von Kleist and his wife in their home. They were Russian aristocrats; if this really was Anastasia it would be very useful to them to have her as their guest. This was to be the first of a long series of homes for her. Somehow she got used to moving from house to house; she had little choice.

Anastasia was a moody person. She could be very pleasant and charming and often was. However, when she was in a bad mood she could be just the opposite. At some time in the past (the night of the assassination?) she had suffered a severe head injury and this could easily account for her difficult moods.

## D > At what times did Anastasia speak Russian?

Through the years Anastasia was questioned many times, most frequently by members of the Russian colony. She disliked these interrogations; however, she realised that they were necessary if she wanted to prove who she was and tried to get used to their many questions.

It was the sincere belief of a number of these aristocrats that the young woman was indeed the Grand Duchess Anastasia. Among their reasons for thinking so were these:
— after just one look into her eyes people who used to be with Anastasia almost daily as a girl were convinced she was the Grand Duchess;
— her handwriting, according to an expert, was exactly like that of the true Anastasia;
— her manner was that of a person who was used to living in an imperial court;
— when talking to Russian aristocrats she brought up many incidents that only the real Anastasia would know about;
— it was true that when she was awake she spoke only German but she was often heard speaking Russian in her sleep;
— many anecdotes demonstrated her validity, such as the day Tatiana, daughter of the Tsar's personal physician, visited her; Anastasia reminded Tatiana of the time she, as a child, had measles and Tatiana helped put her to bed – only the doctor, Tatiana and Anastasia would know about that incident.

People who insisted that the woman was an imposter claimed:
— she spoke only German because she did not know Russian;
— she looked nothing like Anastasia – for one thing, she was too short;
— she was really a Polish girl who had disappeared three days before 'Miss Unknown' was rescued from the canal;
— at times this woman was unable to answer questions that the real Anastasia would be able to reply to automatically;
— Princess Irene of Prussia, aunt of the Grand Duchess Anastasia, said after visiting the young woman that this was not her niece;
— 'Miss Unknown' had no documents or other proof of her identity.

## E   What was Professor Manahan's reason for inviting Anastasia to Charlottesville, Virginia?

In 1928 Princess Xenia, a niece of the Tsar, invited Anastasia to her home in the United States. Her stay with the Russian princess was a happy one. In order to be left alone, unbothered by newspaper reporters, Anastasia took the name of Anna Anderson.

Once again Anastasia became ill and, preferring to be in a German hospital, she returned to Europe. This was in 1931. Eventually she got over her illness, which was tuberculosis, and went to the Bavarian Black Forest to live. Her stay there was a quiet one; she received only those people she wished to see.

In 1933 she began a legal battle involving what she felt was her inheritance. The lawsuit continued for 37 years and became the longest in legal history. Finally, in 1970, it was settled, although not in Anastasia's favour. In the end the Tsar's wealth was distributed among secondary heirs.

In 1968 Anastasia went back to the United States, this time at the invitation of Dr John Manahan, a history professor at the University of Virginia in Charlottesville. He invited her, he said, because he wanted 'to get Anastasia's story written straight.'

On 23 December, 1968, Anastasia became Mrs John Manahan. She spent her remaining years in Charlottesville and, in general, they were not unpleasant years.

By 1970, when she made her last attempt to obtain the Tsar's property, Anastasia was old, tired and ill. Again she failed. 'It no longer matters', she said. 'After all these years I am used to being disappointed. Besides, I know who I am.' She died peacefully on 12 February, 1984. Whether or not she was the Grand Duchess Anastasia, daughter of Tsar Nicholas II, she herself sincerely believed that she was.

# Comprehension check

Some of these statements about Anastasia are true, others are false. Decide whether each statement is true or false and correct the false ones.
1 The Russian colony in Berlin called the young woman 'Miss Unknown'.
2 The doctors found scars all over her body.
3 The Tsar and his family were killed in Ekaterinburg.
4 Anastasia married a soldier named Sergei Tschaikovsky.

53

5 Not everyone was convinced that 'Miss Unknown' was the daughter of the Tsar.

6 Anastasia was always pleasant and courteous to everyone.

7 She changed her name when she went to America because she wanted to be left alone.

8 Princess Irene of Prussia was one of the people who believed this was the real Anastasia.

9 Anastasia lost her legal battle to obtain the Tsar's wealth.

# Language practice

## 1 Vocabulary

Here is some vocabulary from the text. You can deduce the meanings of these words from their context in the reading. In the left-hand column are the words from the reading; on the right are their definitions. Match the words with the definitions. The first one has been done for you.

| | | | | |
|---|---|---|---|---|
| 1 | splash (*l. 2*) **i** | a | shot | |
| 2 | initiated (*l. 3*) | b | those who get property when someone dies | |
| 3 | lawsuit (*l. 4*) | | | |
| 4 | scars (*l. 10*) | c | children's disease resulting in fever and red spots on the skin | |
| 5 | fainted (*l. 25*) | | | |
| 6 | fired (*l. 25*) | d | lost consciousness | |
| 7 | smuggled (*l. 27*) | e | having changes of feelings, eg, sad to happy, happy to sad | |
| 8 | imposter (*l. 50*) | | | |
| 9 | moody (*l. 56*) | f | made an agreement about | |
| 10 | interrogation (*l. 61*) | g | someone pretending to be someone/thing he/she is not | |
| 11 | measles (*l. 78*) | | | |
| 12 | inheritance (*l. 99*) | h | took in or out secretly | |
| 13 | settled (*l. 101*) | i | sound made when something falls into water | |
| 14 | heirs (*l. 102*) | | | |
| | | j | marks left on the skin by an injury | |
| | | k | began | |
| | | l | money/property received after someone's death | |
| | | m | dispute taken to court | |
| | | n | questioning | |

## 2 Phrasal verbs

These phrasal verbs also come from the text. Match them with their definitions.

| | | | |
|---|---|---|---|
| 1 | come out (*l. 19*) | a | recover from an illness |
| 2 | head for (*l. 36*) | b | register (in a hotel, etc.) |
| 3 | check in (*l. 39*) | c | introduce a topic of conversation |
| 4 | account for (*l. 59*) | d | give an explanation for |
| 5 | bring up (*l. 72*) | e | become known |
| 6 | get over (*l. 96*) | f | go in the direction of |

## 3 Grammar: *used to/be used to/get used to*

*After just one look into her eyes people who used to be with Anastasia almost daily were convinced she was the Grand Duchess.*

*Used to* + a simple verb expresses a past state which is no longer true, or a repeated action in the past that no longer happens. The interrogatives and negatives are formed with *did/didn't + use to.*

*Her manner was that of a person who was used to living in an imperial court.*
*Be used to* + a noun form, including gerunds, expresses *be accustomed to, have the habit of.*

*After a time she seemed to get used to hospital life.*
*Get used to* + a noun form, including gerunds, means *become accustomed to, get the habit of.*

### Exercise
Complete the answers to the following questions with a form of *used to, be used to,* or *get used to.*
1 Was Anastasia accustomed to speaking German? No, she _____ .
2 Did it take her long to become accustomed to hospital life? No, it didn't take her long _____ .
3 Was she pretty when she was a girl? Yes, she _____ .
4 Was she accustomed to being with aristocrats? Yes, she _____ .
5 Did she become accustomed to living in different people's homes? Yes, she _____ .
6 As a child did Anastasia live in the Imperial Palace in Moscow? Yes, she _____ .

# Discussion

Your teacher will give you instructions on how to do this part of the lesson.

# Writing

In a short paragraph say why you think 'Miss Unknown' was/was not the Tsar's daughter.

# Index of vocabulary and phrasal verbs

Below are all the words and phrasal verbs that appear in the ten lessons of *Unsolved Mysteries* as new vocabulary. The number following each is that of the unit in which it first appears.

## Vocabulary

abandoned  *3*
aboard  *3*
aerial  *5*
aircraft  *5*
aliens  *5*
anecdotes  *6*
archaeologists  *4*
asthma  *9*
authentic  *2*
axe  *7*

bank  *4*
barn  *7*
become aware  *8*
below decks  *3*
beneath  *2*
bitter  *9*
blasted  *1*

celebrity  *9*
claim  *1*
cone-shaped  *6*
contradicting  *7*
crew  *3*

deserted  *3*
disclose  *9*
dispute  *2*
distorted  *6*
ditch  *4*
diver  *2*

eclipse  *4*
emerge  *5*

excessive  *8*
extraterrestrial  *8*
eye witness  *1*

fainted  *10*
features  *6*
fired  *10*
first mate  *3*
fled  *2*
flippers  *1*
foam  *1*
fuel  *8*
fulfilled  *9*

glaciers  *1*
graveyard  *8*
groan  *7*

heirs  *10*
hind  *6*
huge  *1*

imposter  *10*
inheritance  *10*
inhibited  *7*
initiated  *10*
interrogation  *10*

jury  *7*

lawsuit  *10*
logbook  *3*
logs  *1*
mass
    hallucination  *1*

measles  *10*
meteorites  *5*
monks  *5*
moody  *10*
motive  *7*
mutiny  *3*

nap  *7*
nickname  *9*
nodded  *6*

otters  *1*

pessimistic  *9*
phases  *4*
phenomena  *5*
plain  *4*
pottery  *4*

rafts  *4*
rebel  *9*
relics  *6*
remains  *8*
resented  *7*
reward  *6*
routine  *8*

sank  *2*
sarcasm  *9*
scalp  *6*
scars  *10*
settled  *10*
settlers  *6*
sharks  *3*

sightings  *5*
skimming  *5*
sledge  *4*
smuggled  *10*
species  *6*
speculation  *2*
splash  *10*
stared  *1*
steering  *3*
stepmother  *7*
straits  *2*
struggled  *7*
sulphur  *8*
summer solstice  *4*

temple  *4*
threat  *5*
tidal wave  *2*
torrid  *7*
trace  *8*
turn of the
    century  *9*

upright  *6*

vanished  *9*
verdict  *7*
visionary  *2*
voyage  *3*

weird  *8*
wounded  *9*
worshipped  *4*

## Phrasal verbs

account for  *10*

blow up  *2*
break out  *9*
bring up  *10*

carry out  *9*
catch on  *6*
check in  *10*
come round  *7*
come forward  *6*
come out  *10*
come upon  *2*

do away with  *5*
drop off  *6*

explain away  *5*

find out  *2*

get away  *6*
get back  *2*
get over  *10*
get rid of  *6*
go along with  *2*
go around  *9*
go down  *8*
go on  *1*

head for  *10*
hear from  *9*
hush up  *8*

laugh off  *1*
let up  *3*
line up  *4*
look over  *5*

make out  *3*
make up  *3*
mistake for  *5*

name after  *4*

pass away  *7*
pop up  *1*
put out  *1*
put up  *4*

run away with  *6*

run into  *6*
run out of  *8*

settle down  *9*
sign over  *7*
stretch out  *7*

take off  *8*
take over  *3*
touch up  *1*
turn down  *7*
turn into  *4*
turn over  *8*
turn up  *3*

wash up  *3*